PRAISE FOR
HOW TO BE TOTALLY MISERABLE

"In his insightful new book, *How to Be Totally Miserable*, John Bytheway uniquely describes the consequences of our choices in easy-to-swallow bites that taste real and ring true. Once again, Bytheway hits the nail directly on the head for teens."

—Sean Covey, author of *7 Habits of Highly Effective Teens*

"Who knew such a *miserable* book could be so uplifting and helpful! The gems of wisdom and timeless quotes John Bytheway has compiled provide a powerful antidote to misery, as well as an effective guide to happiness. Teens and adults alike will benefit from this little 'big' book."

—Jill C. Manning, Ph.D., Licensed Marital & Family Therapist

"John Bytheway's wit, humor, and wisdom are apparent in this book. He realizes that we are often just a thought away from making a decision to live our lives differently. I find his words inspiring and encouraging."

—Dr. James MacArthur, author of *Everyday Parents Raising Great Kids*

HOW TO BE Totally Miserable

HOW TO BE Totally Miserable

Miserable

A Self-Hinder Book

JOHN BYTHEWAY

SHADOW
MOUNTAIN

© 2007 John Bytheway

Visit us at ShadowMountain.com

Library of Congress Cataloging-in-Publication Data on file

ISBN 978-1-59038-743-6 (pbk. : alk. paper)

Printed in the United States of America
Malloy Lithographing Incorporated, Ann Arbor, MI

20   19   18   17

Dedicated to the miserable,
the happy, and all those in between
who can't decide which
they want to be

Daily, constantly, we choose by our desires, our thoughts, and our actions whether we want to be blessed or cursed, happy or miserable.

—Ezra Taft Benson

INTRODUCTION

They say that in life suffering is mandatory, but misery is optional.

We all have problems, but we also have choices. We can choose to be happy, or we can choose to be miserable.

Being miserable requires effort—you have to ignore a lot of things.

In this little book, you'll learn how to be miserable, and on the way, you'll also learn how not to be. (Miserable, that is . . .)

You've heard of the French Nation? or the British Nation?—Well, this is the Imagi-Nation.

—Kris Kringle, *Miracle on 34th Street*

Real difficulties can be overcome; it is the imaginary ones that are unconquerable.

—Theodore N. Vail

Imagination is more important than knowledge.

—Albert Einstein

USE YOUR IMAGI-NATION TO WORRY

The Imagi-Nation is a little country in your head. When you're young, you go there to play. When you get older, you go there to plan. But the miserable use the Imagi-Nation for only one thing—they go there to *worry*. Worrywarts are mountains on the relief map of the Imagi-Nation. Faith is like Compound W. It is prescription-strength medicine for worrywarts. But the miserable listen to their doubts more than their faith. To remain miserable, you must visit the Imagi-Nation only to worry. You mustn't go there to dream, ponder, or play. Miserable people go to the Imagi-Nation to act out all the bad things that might happen. Their Imagi-Nation is nothing but an endless marathon of worst-case scenarios. Using your imagination to worry will also ensure that you remain alone—no one wants to be around a worrywart, because worrywarts are contagious.

3

Change the way you look at things, and the things you look at change.

—Wayne Dyer

Change your thoughts and you change the world.

—Norman Vincent Peale

Tough times never last, but tough people do!

—Robert Schuller

BELIEVE THAT THINGS WILL NEVER CHANGE

The sun goes up, and the sun goes down. Seasons come and seasons go. The rain falls in the spring; the summer sun shines; the weather turns cool, then cold. The clouds gather, and the snow flies. Everything in nature goes through cycles. If you're in the midst of a trial, things will change. If your heart aches, it will heal. Those striving to be miserable must ignore all this. They must believe that things will *never* change, that the sun will *not* come out tomorrow, that the clouds don't have a silver lining, and that they *don't* deserve a break today. The miserable believe that nothing *ever* changes, ever! (Okay, change the page.)

Whenever he thought about it, he felt ter-
rible. And so, at last, he came to a fateful
decision. He decided not to think about it.

—John-Roger and Peter McWilliams

Everyone can be discontented if he
ignores his blessings and looks only at his
burdens.

—Thomas S. Monson

THINK ABOUT YOUR PROBLEMS

In order to be miserable, you're going to have to spend a lot of time thinking about your problems. Sure, there are lots of much more interesting things to think about, like your plans, your goals, your dreams—and, like the song says, when you are worried and you can't sleep, you might even count your blessings instead of sheep. But that will only lead to excitement, anticipation, and gratitude. The happiest people think their thoughts according to a plan, and in order to be miserable, you've got to have a plan too—plan to ignore all your wonderful opportunities and ponder only your problems. People eventually become what they think about, so to be miserable, think about your problems, your failures, and your disappointments until you become nothing but a lumbering blob of depression with legs. (Rest assured, however, that if you become a walking problem, someone is going to come along and try to solve you.)

Arise; for this matter belongeth unto thee: ... be of good courage, and do it.

—Ezra 10:4, Old Testament

I think I did pretty well, considering I started out with nothing but a bunch of blank paper.

—Steve Martin

While one person hesitates because he feels inferior, the other is busy making mistakes and becoming superior.

—Henry C. Link

DON'T DO ANYTHING

Miserable people wallow. They just sit there. They don't have a "Things to Do" list, they have a "Things to Don't" list. They don't "go and do," they sit and stew. All their "get up and go" got up and went. Happy people know that *activity and depression are opposites*. They're always out doing something. They're making people laugh, and smile, and say, "I love that guy." They can't wait to get up in the morning because they have places to go and people to see before they go down at night. In order to be miserable, it's important that you don't have any accomplishments to think about when your head hits the pillow. The miserable would rather worry than work. The motto of the miserable is "Just Don't Do It."

Anyone who is really happy must not be paying attention.

—Unknown

He who worries about calamities suffers them twice over.

—Og Mandino

WORRY ABOUT THINGS YOU CAN'T CONTROL

There are problems in the Middle East, the killer bees are migrating northward, there's not enough snowpack in the mountains, and your team is out of the playoffs. This is a small list—if you want a bigger one, watch the evening news. Keep a list of all the sad, dismal, sordid, and ugly events so you know exactly how depressed to be. Then you can mope and worry and fret and be glum. If you want to be miserable, worry about things over which you have no control. Happy people do exactly the opposite. Happy people do their part, do their best, then let go and let God do the rest. They do what they can within their circle of influence. This approach is the opposite of misery, since it will only lead to faith and optimism.

I complained because I had no shoes until I saw a man who had no feet.

—Sign in a shoe repair shop

COMPLAIN ABOUT YOUR BLESSINGS

Lots of people complain. Most people complain about their problems, but miserable people are different—they complain about their *blessings*. If their car breaks down, they complain that it isn't new. If their waitress is slow, they complain and withhold a tip. If their cell phone drops a call, they complain about their service. They're like the people in the Old Testament who got free food from heaven and said, "What? Manna again?" By contrast, happy people are grateful to have a car, thankful they can afford to eat at a restaurant, and stoked that they have a cell phone. Most people in the world don't have cars, can't afford restaurants, and have never sent a text message. Happy people count their blessings, while the miserable complain about theirs.

It is one of the beautiful compensations of life that no man can sincerely try to help another without helping himself.

—Ralph Waldo Emerson

Generally speaking, the most miserable people I know are those who are obsessed with themselves; the happiest people I know are those who lose themselves in the service of others.

—Gordon B. Hinckley

THINK ABOUT YOURSELF

Miserable people think about their height, their weight, their hair, their car, their clothes, their nose. They live in a world of their own. They say things like, "But enough about me . . . what do you think about me?" They treat people like things and things like people. They run their own 24-7 self-service station. Happy people know that the key to being happy is making others so. They see every new day as another opportunity to make the world a better place by making a difference to others. Miserable people think of others only when comparing themselves to them. And when they compare themselves to others, they become either vain or bitter (or more miserable).

Your imagination is yours. You can remember the past you choose, rehearse the future you want, and identify with the real and fictional heroes and events of your selection.

—John-Roger and Peter McWilliams

RELIVE YOUR BAD MEMORIES

There you are, faced with a pile of videos labeled "memories," and a VCR called your brain. Hmmm, which tape should you play? It depends on whether you're trying to be happy or miserable. If you're trying to be happy, play the ones that give you hope and make you laugh! If you're trying to be miserable, play and replay the tapes of your past mistakes. Relive all the less-than-good times as if they had value. It's a ridiculous strategy, but that's what miserable people do. As with all other video selections, you have a choice. Happy people sometimes replay a sad memory, but they have the motto, "Be kind, don't rewind." If they've done something stupid in their past, they repent, refocus, rewind, and re-record something else over that bad memory. As Stephen R. Covey might say, "They live out of their imagination, not out of their memory." Miserable people watch the tape again and again until they're depressed. They don't realize that their past doesn't define their future.

When people point fingers at someone else, they should remember that three fingers are pointing back at them.

—Old saying

If you could kick the person responsible for most of your troubles, you wouldn't be able to sit down for six months.

—Unknown

This is the true joy in life, the being used for a purpose recognized by yourself as a mighty one; the being thoroughly worn out before you are thrown on the scrap heap; the being a force of Nature instead of a feverish selfish little clod of ailments and grievances complaining that the world will not devote itself to making you happy.

—George Bernard Shaw

BLAME EVERYONE AND EVERYTHING

Miserable people are medalists at the annual Blame Games. They are world-class winners in whining, bronze medalists in buck-passing, and victors in victimhood. They hurdle their classes and blame their teachers for their grades; they javelin their jobs and blame their genes; they backstroke through their blessings and blame their background. They say, "It's the school's fault, the government's fault, the weather's fault, my birth-order's fault, my bed's fault. (I got up on the wrong side of it)." They run an "it's not my fault" marathon, and at the closing ceremony they close their minds. Their national anthem says, "o'er the land of the free (free from responsibility) and the home of the blame."

This one makes a net;
This one stands and wishes.
Would you like to bet
Which one gets the fishes?

—Chinese rhyme

Be not afraid of growing slowly,
be afraid only of standing still.

—Chinese proverb

DON'T TAKE ANY ACTION

Some things in this world act, and others are acted upon. Happy people act. Miserable people are acted upon. Thinking about your problems without doing anything about them will ensure that you remain miserable and emotionally groggy. People who jog or take a walk around the block know that moving around and getting their blood flowing somehow gives their brain the energy to sort out all the stuff that's going on. Sometimes even mowing the lawn is great therapy for getting depression off your turf. Happy people get the sun in their hair and the wind in their face. They listen to the birds, smell the flowers, feel the breeze, and suddenly things seem a little better. Those who feel miserable inside often stay inside; those who want to get the misery out of themselves get themselves out of the house and find something to do.

Our doubts are traitors,
   And makes us lose the good we
oft might win,
   By fearing to attempt.
—William Shakespeare

It's hard to fight an enemy who
has outposts in your head.
—Sally Kempton

PUT YOURSELF DOWN

Miserable people put themselves down. If you extend a hand to them, they return a backhand. If you pay them a compliment, they give you a refund! They have a "no, I'm not" for every "yes, you are." It's exhausting to be around them. Every time they put themselves down, you try to lift them up, and the weight becomes too much to bear! Their attitude is not humility, it's humiliating. Happy people know their shortcomings, but they don't sell themselves short. They believe their souls are precious, and when the world weighs them down, they let God lift them up.

People who say that life is not worthwhile are really saying that they themselves have no personal goals which are worthwhile. Get yourself a goal worth working for. Better still, get yourself a project. Always have something ahead of you to "look forward to"—to work for and hope for.

—Maxwell Maltz

DON'T SET GOALS

If you're trying to be miserable, it's important you don't have any goals. No school goals, personal goals, spiritual goals, family goals. With nothing to shoot for, your life is shot. Your only objective each day should be to inhale, exhale, and pump blood. Don't read anything informative; don't listen to anything useful; don't do anything productive. If you start achieving goals, you might start to feel a sense of accomplishment; then you might want to set another goal, and as soon as that happens, your miserable mornings are through. To maintain your misery, the idea of crossing off your achievements should never cross your mind.

All of us carry excess baggage around from time to time, but the wisest ones among us don't carry it for very long. They get rid of it. . . . Often . . . the things we carry are petty, even stupid. If you are still upset after all these years because Aunt Clara didn't come to your wedding reception, why don't you grow up? Forget it.

—Boyd K. Packer

When we hate our enemies, we are giving them power over us: power over our sleep, our appetites, our blood pressure, our health, and our happiness. . . . Our hate is not hurting them at all, but our hate is turning our days and nights into a hellish turmoil.

—Dale Carnegie

HOLD ON TO GRUDGES

Okay, everyone out there who needs to be forgiven for something, raise your hand. Hmmm, it appears the voting is unanimous. But if you want to be miserable, don't ever forgive others. Hold on to a grudge. Grudges sour your mood and ruin your day. Days turn into months and months into years. Carrying a grudge for all that time wastes a lot of energy that could be used for living life to the fullest. You can't hold on to happiness unless you let go of grudges, so to be miserable, don't bury the hatchet. Be mad at everyone and everything, and soon enough the grudges will bury you.

27

"I can't cheer up—I don't WANT to cheer up. It's nicer to be miserable!"

—Anne of Green Gables

It is difficult to make a man miserable while he feels he is worthy of himself and claims kindred to the great God who made him.

—Abraham Lincoln

STAY MISERABLE

Some people are miserable because, well, maybe they enjoy it. Perhaps it's easier to be mad at everyone and everything than to look inside and realize that you don't have to be miserable— or more important, you don't have to *stay* miserable. The fact is, when you get sick and tired of being sick and tired, you'll change. You'll find that it takes work and effort to stay miserable when there's so much to be optimistic about in the world. Ignore all that. Forget that you have friends who care about you and that if you were gone, you would be missed. Forget that you have the potential at any moment to make someone else's day by a smile, a kind word, or a secret act of service. Forget the last time you laughed so hard that milk came out of your nose, forget . . .

Hey, are you beginning to smile? There's nothing funny about wasting dairy products. You have a lot to learn about being miserable. Never mind, turn the page.

Suspicion is the cancer of friendship.

—Francesco Petrarch

Better to be occasionally cheated than perpetually suspicious.

—B. C. Forbes

JUDGE OTHER PEOPLE'S MOTIVES

Miserable people are suspicious. If someone's nice to them, miserable people say, "Hmmm, I wonder why they did that." They look sideways at service and think that angels have an angle. Happy people receive the gift and return gratitude, while the miserable are gracious up front, but wonder what's behind it. Everyone's a suspect, and favors are fishy. They don't realize that the good Samaritans of the world aren't performing acts of kindness because they think they're on camera—they might actually be good! But if you're trying to be miserable, be critical of kindnesses done to you, and believe that everyone has a hidden agenda.

Most folks are about as happy as they make up their minds to be.

—Abraham Lincoln

Happiness is not something you postpone for the future; it is something you design for the present.

—Jim Rohn

PUT DEADLINES
ON YOUR HAPPINESS

Miserable people look for some outside event to make them happy. "As soon as I graduate, I'll be happy." After they graduate, they say, "Well, as soon as I get a job, I'll be happy." After they get a job, they say, "Okay, as soon as I get married, I'll be happy." Miserable people never seem to learn that happiness is a decision, not a destination. It's an attitude, not an event! If you're determined to be miserable, then think of life as a waiting room, and happiness as your doctor. You know you'll be waiting in there forever, so enjoy the magazines. (And when you finally get into see Dr. Happiness, he'll just tell you to schedule another appointment—and *then* you'll be happy.)

Beware of covetousness: for a man's life consisteth not in the abundance of the things which he possesseth.

—Luke 12:15, New Testament

Remember that in the end, surely God will be looking only for clean hands, not full ones.

—Jeffrey R. Holland

A man is rich in proportion to the number of things which he can afford to let alone.

—Henry David Thoreau

ALWAYS WANT MORE

The miserable think that what they have is never enough. Like the Little Mermaid, who owned no fewer than twenty thingamabobs, they say, "But who cares, no big deal, I want *more*." (How could you be miserable with twenty thingamabobs?) The miserable say, "If only I had one of those, I'd be happy." Actually, the more you have, the more you have to worry about—in other words, the more stuff you have, the more the stuff has you! Even Hollywood stars who appear to "have it all" have nothing if they haven't learned how to be content. The only things we can take with us when we die are our character, our intelligence, and our relationships. Everything else falls apart. Clothes attract moths, cars get rusty, and stuff gets stolen. That's why Jesus said, "Lay up for yourselves treasures in heaven, where neither moth nor rust doth corrupt, and where thieves do not break through nor steal" (Matthew 6:20, New Testament).

Most of the shadows of this life are caused by standing in one's own sunshine.

—Ralph Waldo Emerson

BE A BREATH OF
STALE AIR

Some people are fun to be around. When they enter the room, they're like the proverbial "breath of fresh air." Whatever the weather, they're always happy. If the skies aren't blue, they see clouds with silver linings. If there's a storm, they start singing in the rain The miserable, on the other hand, choose to look at every bad thing as if it's happening personally to them. They can always find a way to make things worse. They seem to delight in "throwing a wrench in the works" and "putting a damper on things." No job is fulfilling, no dance has the right music, and no class is sufficiently entertaining. You wish they'd just keep their mouths closed, because all that comes out is stale air (and they're out of Tic Tacs).

Man's mind, once stretched by a new idea, never regains its original dimensions.

—Oliver Wendell Holmes

Some people drink from the fountain of knowledge, others just gargle.

—Robert Newton Anthony

DON'T LEARN
ANYTHING NEW

Happy people love to learn. Miserable people think learning is just too much work. Happy people love getting up in the morning knowing that in the day ahead, they will learn many new things they didn't know when they got up. Happy people are interested, inspiring, and inquisitive. They're also intelligent, because when you ask a lot of questions of others, you're bound to learn something yourself. Miserable people would rather lounge than learn. They use their drive time to tune in to trash, while the happy turn their cars into classrooms. The miserable read only what they have to for the test, and they'd rather take naps than take notes.

Ask, and it shall be given you; seek, and ye shall find; knock, and it shall be opened unto you.

—Matthew 7:7, New Testament

Do not pray for easy lives. Pray to be stronger men! Do not pray for tasks equal to your powers. Pray for power equal to your tasks.

—Phillips Brooks

POSTPONE PRAYER

The happiest people pray early and often, while the miserable often postpone prayer to be used only as a last resort. Happy people keep in touch; miserable people keep their distance until the crisis is on. A teenage girl once said, "Prayer is so easy to stop and so hard to start again—but operators are standing by." In prayer we are never alone, because God plus one other person is a majority, and "if God be for us, who can be against us?" (Romans 8:31, New Testament). Sometimes just knowing the Lord is there and watching over us is a great remedy for misery. Happy people stand tallest when they're on their knees, but the miserable haven't got a prayer.

Instead of waiting for someone
to take you under their wing, go
out there and find a good wing to
climb under.

—Dave Thomas

AVOID GOOD COMPANY

A friend is someone who makes it easier for you to reach your fullest potential. Happy people build, lift, encourage, and motivate, and being in their company always makes you want to be better too. People who are trying to be miserable try to find friends who weigh them down with gloom and doubt. Misery loves this kind of company. Bad company will try to take you to places you shouldn't be and tempt you to do things you shouldn't do. Then, after you've followed their plan of misery, you feel empty inside, and you wonder why you're miserable! Well, perhaps bad feelings accompany bad company.

I know only two tunes: One of them is "Yankee Doodle" and the other isn't.

—Ulysses S. Grant

There is no music in hell, for all good music belongs to heaven.

—Brigham Young

Sing, O heavens; and be joyful, O earth; and break forth into singing, O mountains: for the Lord hath comforted his people, and will have mercy upon his afflicted.

—Isaiah 49:13, Old Testament

DON'T SING

Aria hungry? Let's eat overture place. Sonata bad idea. There's something about singing a song that makes you happy. If happy people have sunshine in their souls, then miserable people must have a black hole in theirs (and people who read a lot of self-help books must have chicken soup in their souls). Have you ever seen a depressed person sing? Miserable people sing the blues, while happy people sing "Blue Skies Shinin' on Me." Happy people sing in the shower, sing in the car, even whistle while they work. Happy people sing "Zip-a-dee doo dah!" while the miserable zip-padee up their mouths.

It takes sixty-four muscles of the face to make a frown, and only thirteen to make a smile. Why work overtime?

—Old saying

The best way to wake up with a smile on your face is to go to bed with one already there.

—Richard C. Miller

Smiling is the second best thing you can do with your mouth.

—Bumper sticker

DON'T SMILE

If you're trying to be miserable, don't smile. Some people are smiling on the inside, but they forget to tell their face. A clever bumper sticker says, "Put a smile on your kisser, and someone may put a kiss on your smiler." (I think I'll put that on the bathroom mirror and see if my wife gets the hint.) I read in the paper that it's a psychological fact that smiling on the outside makes you feel better on the inside (if it's in the paper, it must be true). People who are happy walk with their shoulders back and their heads up. If you want to be miserable, slump your shoulders, look at the ground, go to your unhappy place, and whatever you do, don't smile.

When I was attending college, I enrolled in a physiology class. One day during a lecture the professor asked me to sit up on the high table at the front of the room so he could demonstrate the principle of reflexes. He took a little mallet, similar to the one a medical doctor would use, and proceeded to tap me on the knee, expecting my leg to jerk noticeably in typical reflex action. However, I held my leg very rigid and flipped my arm in the air when he tapped my knee. The class roared with delight. The professor was not amused.

—Boyd K. Packer

Laughter is sunshine; it chases winter from the human face.

—Victor Hugo

Laughter is the closest distance between two people.

—Victor Borge

DON'T LAUGH

Miserable people don't laugh. It might break their concentration! They have important world issues to worry about. Happy people giggle, guffaw, chortle, snicker, and even snort. (Snorters cover their mouths in surprise and embarrassment, and then laugh even harder.) If laughter is the best medicine, these people have free refills at the funny pharmacy. Have you ever laughed so hard that your stomach was sore the next day? There's an exercise program idea in there somewhere: "Laugh Your Way to Washboard Abs." Laughing and smiling are related, and laughing is just smiling out loud. Miserable people think life is too serious to laugh about, while happy people know that life's so serious they have to laugh to survive.

If we could read the secret history of our enemies, we should find in each man's life sorrow and suffering enough to disarm all hostility.

—Henry Wadsworth Longfellow

BACKBITE

Miserable people backbite. They haven't learned that if you want to be big, you shouldn't belittle. Happy people have learned that there is no nobility in confessing the faults of other people behind their backs. Besides, backbiting leaves a bad taste in your mouth. Happy people believe if they judge harshly, they may be judged harshly in return. They speak of what's right with others instead of what's wrong. They'd rather lighten the load on the backs of others than bite them. Happy people keep their teeth to themselves.

Love not sleep, lest thou come to poverty.

—Proverbs 20:13, Old Testament

Some dream of big things, others wake up and do them.

—Old saying

I wish I could stand on a busy corner, hat in hand, and beg people to throw me all their wasted hours.

—Bernard Berenson

SLEEP TOO MUCH

Miserable people think they can escape their problems by sleeping. They think the perfect world is found only on their Perfect Sleeper (that's a mattress brand). Happy people know that one of the purposes of life is to matter—and you can't matter much when you're merged with your mattress. Miserable people repeatedly hit the snooze button to avoid living each day to the fullest. When life's alarm clock goes off and says, "Get up and do something," they smack the snooze button and say, "Yeah, sometime I will." At the end of their lives, when their Creator says, "What did you do with your life?" they'll say, "Well, um, I was kinda tired."

The world turns aside to let any man pass who knows whither he is going.

—David Starr Jordan

I always wanted to be somebody, but I should have been more specific.

—Lily Tomlin

Behold also the ships, which though they be so great, and are driven of fierce winds, yet are they turned about with a very small helm, whithersoever the governor listeth.

—James 3:4, New Testament

DON'T HAVE A PURPOSE

Happy people don't get down, because they have a reason to get up. They know why they're here and what they're supposed to do. Since they have a purpose, they live their life *on purpose*. They memorize their mission, ponder their purpose, and always seem to be going someplace. Having a purpose is like a rudder that steers you through life's storms, winds, and currents. Miserable people drift. They just go with the flow without asking where the flow will go. They don't push through the waves, they get pushed around by them. Miserable people have no plans, no goals, no dreams, no purpose. No wonder they're miserable!

The past is behind; learn from it.
The future is ahead; prepare for it.
The present is here; live in it!

—Thomas S. Monson

Regret is an appalling waste of energy; you can't build on it; it's only good for wallowing in.

—Katherine Mansfield

RECYCLE REGRETS

Miserable people have a recycle bin full of past mistakes. Every day they rethink their regrets and recycle their remorse. Their language is full of phrases like, "I should've," "I would've," "I could've," "Why didn't I?" and "If only." They never look where they're going because they can't take their eyes off where they've been. Happy people know that you can either learn from the past or live in it. (The past is a nice place to visit, but you wouldn't want to live there.) Happy people would rather move on to their future than move in to their past. They turn every regret into a resolve. Rather than saying, "I can't believe I did that," they repent, refocus, and say, "Whew. I'll never do that again!"

For God hath not given us the spirit of fear; but of power, and of love, and of a sound mind.

—2 Timothy 1:7, New Testament

Fear is that little darkroom where negatives are developed.

—Michael Pritchard

TAKE COUNSEL FROM YOUR FEARS

Miserable people always think about what might go wrong. They plan their actions based on their fears. The best they can do is imagine all the worst-case scenarios of what might happen. This is a recipe for misery. Someone once said that FEAR means *False Expectations Appearing Real*. Very often, the things we fear might happen never do. When angels come to earth, they almost always begin their message by saying, "Fear not." I guess it would be pretty frightening to see an angel, but maybe there's something more to what they're saying. Perhaps there's a message about faith in there. Think about it. Angels come from this heavenly place, and the first thing out of their mouth is, "Fear not," as if to say, "You people down on earth are always afraid."

Whenever anyone has offended me, I try to raise my soul so high that the offense cannot reach it.

—René Descartes

We should be too big to take offense, and too noble to give it.

—Abraham Lincoln

BE EASILY OFFENDED

Miserable people take offense. If you say something, it offends them. If you don't say something, it offends them. They're mad when someone tries to help, and they're mad when someone doesn't. They're even offended when someone is trying to make amends! They're offended if someone apologizes too late, too quickly, or not enough. (They might even be offended if someone writes a book about being miserable. Uh-oh.) The happiest people in the world refuse to be offended by everyone and everything. That's just too much work. They forgive quickly because they know they need forgiveness from others.

Many people die with their music still in them. Why is this so? Too often it is because they are always getting ready to live. Before they know it, time runs out.

—Oliver Wendell Holmes

I couldn't wait for success, so I went ahead without it.

—Jonathan Winters

It took me fifteen years to discover I had no talent for writing, but I couldn't give it up because by that time I was too famous.

—Robert Benchley

WAIT FOR LIFE TO HAPPEN

Miserable people are waiting for the world to make them happy. They think there's something wrong if people and things and circumstances aren't going to great lengths to ensure their happiness. But happy people know that the responsibility for being happy is on their own shoulders. They understand the old Chinese proverb, "He who waits for roast duck to fly into mouth must wait a very long time." If you want life to give you a roast duck, or even a small order of fries, remember: You've got to go out and get it! Happiness doesn't deliver.

Life is either a daring adventure or nothing.

—Helen Keller

What would you attempt to do, if you knew you could not fail?

—Robert Schuller

AVOID ADVENTURE

When you ask miserable people, "What's new?" they say, "Nothing." Miserable people haven't done anything new in years. Happy people love to try new things. And when they encounter a problem, they think of it as just another adventure. If they get lost on their way somewhere, they say, "All right, an adventure!" When the power goes out, they gather the flashlights and tell stories on the couch. If they get caught in a cloudburst, they jump in puddles and sing in the rain! Miserable people, on the other hand, don't see an opportunity for adventure, they just think they're being picked on. They ask, "What did I do to deserve this?" or "Why does this always happen to me?" (Oh, be serious, does this *always* happen to you?) Happy people turn little adversities into big adventures.

At the moment of depression, if you will follow a simple program, you will get out of it. Get on your knees and get the help of God, then get up and go find somebody who needs something that you can help them with. Then it will be a good day.

—Marion D. Hanks

No one is useless in this world who lightens the burdens of it for another.

—Charles Dickens

ASSUME THAT MOPING WILL SOLVE THE PROBLEM

Miserable people figure that if they lie around, and stew, and think, and nap, and remove themselves from the world, eventually their doing nothing will solve the problem. Happy people know that misery exits when you enter the life of someone else and make a difference. Ironically, one of the best ways to lift your spirits is to forget yourself and lift someone else's. And, if you'd like a double dose of depression-destroying activity, do something for someone else *anonymously*. There's a certain giggly giddiness that comes your way when you commit random acts of kindness and nobody knows who did it. It's hard to keep frowning when you know someone else is smiling because of you.

STIRRING SUMMARY COMING IN 3 ... 2 ... 1 ...

Well, you've done it. You've finished this book. You must realize that this is in direct violation of the principles outlined on pages 9, 21, and 39. You've done something, you've taken action, and you may have learned something new. In other words, you've taken three steps backwards on the path to becoming miserable. Just don't let it happen again. Studies have shown that people who read books or listen to audio programs about becoming happier, healthier, and more successful tend to become happier, healthier, and more successful. So you must stop it right now.

Okay, let's review: How do you become totally miserable?

Use Your Imagi-Nation to Worry
Believe That Things Will Never Change
Think about Your Problems
Don't Do Anything

Worry about Things You Can't Control
Complain about Your Blessings
Think about Yourself
Relive Your Bad Memories
Blame Everyone and Everything
Don't Take Any Action
Put Yourself Down
Don't Set Goals
Hold On to Grudges
Stay Miserable
Judge Other People's Motives
Put Deadlines on Your Happiness
Always Want More
Be a Breath of Stale Air
Don't Learn Anything New
Postpone Prayer
Avoid Good Company

Don't Sing
Don't Smile
Don't Laugh
Backbite

Sleep Too Much
Don't Have a Purpose
Recycle Regrets
Take Counsel from Your Fears
Be Easily Offended
Wait for Life to Happen
Avoid Adventure
Assume That Moping Will Solve the Problem

(You may need to review this list from time to time to remain a permanent resident of the pit of despair.)

So there you have it. You've just learned how to be totally miserable. But there is a risk—you've also learned how not to be.

SOURCES

Anthony, Robert Newton. www.quoteworld.
org/quotes/469 [accessed 2/20/07].

Benchley, Robert. In *The Writer's Quotation
Book*. Edited by James Charlton. New York:
Penguin Books, 1992, 56.

Benson, Ezra Taft. "The Great Commandment—
Love the Lord," *Ensign*, May 1988, 6.

Berenson, Bernard. In *Inspirations and Insights*.
Compiled by William Arthur Ward. JII / Sales
Promotions Associates, 1994, 253.

Borge, Victor. www.quotationspage.com/quote/
26170.html [accessed 2/20/07].

Brooks, Phillips. www.thinkexist.com [accessed
2/20/07].

Carnegie, Dale. *How to Stop Worrying and Start
Living*. New York: Simon & Schuster, 2004,
111–12.

Chinese rhyme. In *The Forbes Book of Business
Quotations*. Edited by Ted Goodman. New
York: Black Dog and Leventhal Publishers,
1997, 919.

Covey, Stephen R. *The 7 Habits of Highly Effective People* (New York: Simon & Schuster, 1989), 105.

Descartes, René. www.answers.com/topic/renedescartes [accessed 2/20/07].

Dickens, Charles. In *The Forbes Book of Business Quotations*. Edited by Ted Goodman. New York: Black Dog and Leventhal Publishers, 1997, 203.

Dyer, Wayne. *The Power of Intention*. Carlsbad, Calif.: Hay House, 2004, 173.

Einstein, Albert. Quoted in John-Roger and Peter McWilliams, *Life 101*. Los Angeles: Prelude Press, 1990, 150.

Emerson, Ralph Waldo (page 14). www.quoteworld.org/quotes/ 4503 [accessed 2/20/07].

———— (page 36). Quoted in *Bits and Pieces*, March 27, 1997, 19.

Forbes, B. C. www.quotationsbook.com/quotes/38034/ [accessed 2/20/07].

Grant, Ulysses S. In *The Forbes Book of Business Quotations*. Edited by Ted Goodman. New York: Black Dog and Leventhal Publishers, 1997, 601.

Hanks, Marion D. "Make It a Good Day!" *BYU Speeches of the Year, 1966.* Provo, Utah: Brigham Young University, 1967, 6–7.

Hinckley, Gordon B. *Teachings of Gordon B. Hinckley.* Salt Lake City: Deseret Book, 1997, 589.

Holland, Jeffrey R. "Graduation Gifts from the Grave." BYU commencement address, April 26, 1991.

Holmes, Oliver Wendell (page 38). www.quote garden.com/ learning.html [accessed 2/20/07].

———— (page 62). www.quotedb.com/quotes/ 2359 [accessed 2/20/07].

Hugo, Victor. *Les Misérables.* New York: Signet, 1987, 569.

Jordan, David Starr. *The Care and Culture of Men.* N.p., 1896, 7.

Keller, Helen. In *The Forbes Book of Business Quotations.* Edited by Ted Goodman. New York: Black Dog and Leventhal Publishers, 1997, 523.

Kempton, Sally. Quoted in John-Roger and Peter McWilliams, *Do It!* Los Angeles: Prelude Press, 1991, 22.

Lincoln, Abraham (page 28). *Lincoln: Selected Speeches and Writings*. New York: First Vintage Books, 1991, 340.

———— (page 32). *The Wit and Wisdom of Abraham Lincoln*. Compiled by James C. Hume. New York: Gramercy Books, 1999, 19.

———— (page 60). www.dailycelebrations.com/character. htm [accessed 2/20/07].

Link, Henry C. Quoted in John-Roger and Peter McWilliams, *Life 101*. Los Angeles: Prelude Press, 1990, 284.

Longfellow, Henry Wadsworth. *Longfellow: Poems and Other Writings*. New York: Penguin, 2000, 797.

Maltz, Maxwell. Quoted in *The Best of Success: A Treasury of Success Ideas*. Compiled by Wynn Davis. Lombard, Ill.: Great Quotations Pub., 1988, 208.

Mandino, Og. *The Greatest Success in the World*. New York: Bantam Books, 1981, 79.

Manfield, Katherine. In *The Forbes Book of Business Quotations*. Edited by Ted Goodman. New York: Black Dog and Leventhal Publishers, 1997, 778.

Martin, Steve. In *The Writer's Quotation Book*. Edited by James Charlton. New York: Penguin Books, 1992, 67.

McWilliams, John-Roger and Peter (page 6). *Life 101*. Los Angeles: Prelude Press, 1990, 176.

—————— (page 16). *Do It!* Los Angeles: Prelude Press, 1991, 119.

Miller, Richard C. In *Inspirations and Insights*. Compiled by William Arthur Ward. JII / Sales Promotions Associates, 1994, 63.

Monson, Thomas S. (page 6). *Favorite Quotations from the Collection of Thomas S. Monson*. Salt Lake City: Deseret Book, 1985, 142.

—————— (page 56). *Favorite Quotations from the Collection of Thomas S. Monson*. Salt Lake City: Deseret Book, 1985, 140.

Montgomery, Lucy Maud. *Anne of Green Gables*. New York: HarperCollins Publishers, 1999, 357.

Packer, Boyd K. (page 26). *That All May Be Edified*. Salt Lake City: Bookcraft, 1982, 68.

—————— (page 48). *Teach Ye Diligently*. Salt Lake City: Deseret Book, 1975, 212.

Peale, Norman Vincent.
www.leadershipnow.com/ attitudequotes.html
[accessed 2/20/07].

Petrarch, Francesco. thinkexist.com [accessed
2/20/07].

Pritchard, Michael. Quoted in John-Roger and
Peter McWilliams, *Do It!* Los Angeles:
Prelude Press, 1991, 36.

Rohn, Jim. www.jimrohn.com/ezineArchives/
2005/320.asp [accessed 2/20/07].

Schuller, Robert (page 4). *Tough Times Never
Last, but Tough People Do!* Nashville: Thomas
Nelson Publishers, 1983.

———— (page 64). Quoted in John-Roger and
Peter McWilliams, *Life 101.* Los Angeles:
Prelude Press, 1990, 364.

Shakespeare, William. *Measure for Measure,* act
1, scene 4, lines 77–79.

Shaw, George Bernard. *The Wisdom of Bernard
Shaw.* Edited by Charlotte Shaw. New York:
Brentano's, 1913, 51.

Thomas, Dave. Quoted in Cynthia Kersey,
Unstoppable. Naperville, Ill.: Sourcebooks,
1998, 211.

Tomlin, Lily. Quoted in Cynthia Kersey, *Unstoppable*. Naperville, Ill.: Sourcebooks, 1998, 40.

Thoreau, Henry David. *Walden and Other Writings of Henry David Thoreau*. Edited by Brooks Atkinson. New York: Random House, 1992, 77.

Vail, Theodore N. In *The Forbes Book of Business Quotations*. Edited by Ted Goodman. New York: Black Dog and Leventhal Publishers, 1997, 205.

Winters, Jonathan. In *Bits and Pieces*, May 22, 1997, 3.

Young, Brigham. *Discourses of Brigham Young*. Selected by John A. Widtsoe. Salt Lake City: Deseret Book, 1971, 242.

ABOUT THE AUTHOR

John Bytheway is an author and speaker who has given thousands of seminars at schools, hospitals, businesses, and churches. He has traveled around the world and witnessed firsthand that people from Germany to Japan, and from Manchester to Manila can be just as miserable or just as happy as they want to be. He loves to golf and spend time with his children, and can often be found watching *The Andy Griffith Show* and laughing out loud at Deputy Sheriff Barney Fife.

NEW FOR TEENS!

WHAT'S IN *YOUR* BACKPACK?
... a poor self-image?
... a tendency to feel sorry for yourself?
... bad habits?

In this laugh-out-loud, motivational presentation, author and comedian John Bytheway will tell you how to dump the junk and fill your backpack with the things we really need—a capacity to love, a desire to serve, and the energy to make a difference in someone else's life.

ISBN 978-1-59038-770-2
UPC 783027002799
DVD, $19.95
Available at Amazon.com and other national retailers.

What's in Your
Backpack?

Life's a Hike, Travel Light

John Bytheway